Ethereum

Understand the Ethereum Platform, Ether-Mining, Gas and Investment Considerations

Copyright ©2018 by (Tom J. Bernstein)

All rights reserved. No part of this book may be reproduced or transmitted in any form or by any means without written permission from the author.

ISBN-13: 978-1986342414

ISBN-10: 1986342417

Table of Contents

Introduction 1

Chapter 1- Ethereum Basics 2

    What is Ethereum? 2

    What is Ether? 3

    Who Created Ethereum? 5

    What are Smart Contracts? 6

    What is Ethereum Virtual Machine (EVM)? 7

    What is a Decentralized Application (Dapp)? 8

    What is a Decentralized Autonomous Organization (DAO)? 9

    What Makes Ethereum Valuable? 9

Chapter 2- Getting Started with Ethereum 15

Chapter 3- Buying and Selling Ethereum 19

    Buying Ethereum 19

    Ethereum (ETH) vs. Ethereum Classic (ETC) 19

    Buying Ethereum on an Exchange 20

    Buying Ethereum via Peer-to-Peer Trade 23

    Privacy and Security 25

    Purchasing Ethereum Anonymously 26

    Selling Ethereum 26

Chapter 4- Ethereum Wallets 29

    Mobile Wallets 30

    Hardware Wallets 31

Desktop Wallets 31

Paper Wallets 31

Chapter 5- Ethereum Mining 33

How Ethereum Mining Works 34

Shift to proof of stake 36

Selecting Mining Hardware 36

The Mining Software 37

Install Ethminer 38

Join a Mining Pool 39

Chapter 6- Ethereum for Investment 41

Buying and Holding Ethereum 42

Trading Ethereum 43

Buying and Diversifying 43

Mining Ethereum 43

Chapter 7- Securing Ethereum 45

Chapter 8- Developing Dapps on the Ethereum Platform 51

Ethereum Environment Setup 52

Understanding the Gas 54

Chapter 9- Impact of Ethereum to the Economy 56

Chapter 10- The Future of Ethereum Blockchain 61

Chapter 11- Will Ethereum Overtake Bitcoin 66

Chapter 12- Hard Forks 70

Conclusion 75

Introduction

You must have heard of cryptocurrencies by now and how they are changing the economy worldwide. They are simply a kind of digital money that facilitates payments to online. A good feature of cryptocurrency is that it is not controlled by any centralized authority such as a government or a central bank. Cryptocurrencies are also known for facilitating an easy and fast way of making payments. When paying with cryptocurrencies, a small fee is charged per transaction. These are some of the reasons why many people, companies and institutions are turning to cryptocurrencies as opposed to fiat currency. Ethereum is one of the several cryptocurrencies of the world.

Ethereum goes beyond a cryptocurrency by providing a platform with all tools users need to create and run decentralized applications. Decentralized applications are those that can run without depending on a centralized authority. It is easy to create such applications on the Ethereum platforms using high-level a programming language such as Serpent and Solidity.

Chapter 1- Ethereum Basics

What is Ethereum?

Blockchain technology is only known to be applicable to cryptocurrencies such as Bitcoin. However, the fact is there are several other applications of blockchain technology. Cryptocurrencies are just one of many. Ethereum is simply a platform for developers to create decentralized applications (Dapps). The platform runs on blockchain technology. This means that blockchain is the technology underlying Ethereum.

The development of blockchain applications has been a complex process. Individuals who had earlier ventured into this area had a strong background in computer programming, security, cryptography and mathematics. However, Ethereum has changed this completely. It has made the process of developing decentralized applications much easier. This has been achieved by providing developers with the tools necessary for one to develop a decentralized application. It is now easy to develop and deploy a decentralized application.

Bitcoin is well known as a digital currency. It is simply an electronic cash system that supports payments in a peer-to-peer manner. Yes, Ethereum can also be used for this purpose through its tokens are known as *Ether*. However, Ethereum goes beyond this to provide developers and programmers with a platform where they can write programming code for any type of decentralized application. This means that it offers a feature not provided by Bitcoin. Due to this, Ethereum has a bright future and may overtake Bitcoin.

What is Ether?

Ethereum is a public and distributed blockchain technology. The platform is fueled by a cryptographic token known as *Ether*. The users who join the Ethereum network are expected to work to earn this token. Ether is a cryptocurrency just like bitcoin, but it is also used by developers when paying transaction fees on the network.

The goal of Ethereum is to work like a decentralized Internet and a decentralized app store, which leads to the support of a new application known as Dapp (Decentralized application). No one can claim to own Ethereum, hence this functionality is not provided for free. The platform needs Ether which is a unique piece of code that can be used for payment of computing resources needed for running such applications. The Ether is simply a digital bearer asset and no one is required to approve a transaction when paying via Ether.

Instead of functioning like a payment or digital currency, the purpose of Ether is to provide the decentralized applications running on the network with fuel. This is the fuel that will keep these applications running. You can think of this in the way that tokens power user experience. Another example is a decentralized online notebook. For you to post delete or modify a note, you are expected to pay a fee via Ether so that the transaction can be processed.

Due to this, the Ether is referred to as "digital oil". The fee that paid for an Ethereum transaction is calculated based on the amount of "gas" required to process the transaction. Each action performed by a user consumes an amount of gas depending on the amount of time it takes to run as well as the computing resources used. If the transaction costs 400 gas, this must be paid in Ether.

Bitcoin has a market cap limit of 21 million. This is not the case with Ether as it has no market cap. At most eighteen million Ether are mined every year. Whenever a miner discovers a new block, he is rewarded with five Ethers which immediately get into circulation. Currently, no one knows the total amount of Ether in circulation. The rate at which Ether is created is expected to become unclear when a new proof-of-stake algorithm is introduced. The rules of creating Ether will also change as well as the amount of subsidy earned after discovering a new block.

Who Created Ethereum?

Bitcoin was created in 2008 by an anonymous person(s) going by the pseudonym, Satoshi Nakamoto. The goal of developing Bitcoin, as stated in the Whitepaper, was to provide a peer-to-peer electronic cash system for facilitating digital payments. After four years, a 14-year old programmer from Toronto used the same concept employed by Bitcoin in an effort to transform how the Internet operates. Vitalik Buterin first developed his interest in Bitcoin in 2011. In the same year, he founded Bitcoin Magazine, a website for news in which he published several articles about cryptocurrencies.

After some time, he came up with the idea of creating a new platform that will introduce new features not found in Bitcoin. In 2013, he released a whitepaper that described a platform that will support any kind of decentralized application that programmers may want to create. This system was named *Ethereum*. Ethereum has also introduced a new feature known as smart contracts, pieces of code that developers can create and execute automatically when certain conditions are met.

After Buterin had written and published the Ethereum whitepaper, he was joined by other developers. Dr Gavin Wood, a Co-founder then wrote the Ethereum yellow paper which has all the technical specifications for Ethereum. Joseph Lubin, a co-founder focused on Brooklyn-based ConsenSys, which is simply a startup with a focus development of Dapps. In 2014, a crowdfunding campaign was launched that helped them raise Ether, which acts as shares on the network.

The campaign saw them raise a total of $18m, leaving a legacy as the highest amount raised via a crowdfunding campaign at that time. The smart contracts platform then kicked off a year later and has grown a great deal, attracting hundreds of developers and even the tech giants such as Microsoft and IBM.

What are Smart Contracts?

In Ethereum, a smart contract is simply a piece of code executed once a particular condition becomes true. You can create a smart contract to send a particular amount of Ether to a certain recipient on a particular date. When that date is reached, the Ether will be sent automatically without you having to interfere. Due to this, smart contracts are normally used for exchanging anything that has value such as Ether. Smart contracts have contributed a lot to the popularity and adoption of the Ethereum blockchain. It is a feature that many organizations have wanted for a long period of time.

Blockchain implementations such as Bitcoin are known to have a number of limitations imposed on what users can do. Ethereum has changed this by giving blockchain users a degree of freedom not offered in other blockchains. Users are allowed to write code that will help them do whatever they need to do.

What is Ethereum Virtual Machine (EVM)?

Before Ethereum, there was Bitcoin and other blockchain implementations. However, these had imposed some limitations on what users could do. Bitcoin, for example, was only developed to act as a digital currency, facilitating peer-to-peer payments. Users could do nothing more with it.

Developers discovered a problem with this type of implementation. They had to change it. The only way was to change and add more functionalities to Bitcoin or come up with a new implementation of blockchain technology that would offer the features they needed. This led to Vitalik Buterin coming up with the idea of Ethereum.

The Ethereum Virtual Machine, commonly written as EVM is a software that runs on the Ethereum network. The purpose of this software is to allow developers to write and run any type of code on the platform regardless of the programming language used. The EVM is one of the Ethereum features that has greatly contributed to its success. Instead of having to create a new blockchain for every application needed to develop, Ethereum's EVM makes it possible for us to create numerous blockchain applications on a similar platform.

What is a Decentralized Application (Dapp)?

Ethereum is similar to a decentralized appstore where one can publish the Dapps without the need for services of a middleman for management of the information they have. Dapps normally connects their users directly without relying on the services of a middleman. Twitter operates like a decentralized application as no one, including the company, can delete a post once it has been published.

What is a Decentralized Autonomous Organization (DAO)?

You must have heard of the idea of a driverless car powered by artificial intelligence. This is a car that can move without the control of a human driver. The car is capable of searching for passengers, picking them up and dropping them off at their various destinations. This was the idea behind the development of Bitcoin.

Bitcoin was developed to facilitate payments without relying on middlemen. The transacting parties can pay each other directly without a middleman. This means that the purpose of DAOs is to hard-code some of the company rules. DAOs provide us with a way of enforcing company rules digitally.

Note that DAO works based on smart contracts. Once a smart contract or DAO has been deployed into the Ethereum network, no one can change it, which is a great advantage as no single individual can change the rules.

What Makes Ethereum Valuable?

Ethereum is not under the control of a central bank or any government. At the same time, no government or bank can claim that it prints Ethereum. Despite this, Ethereum has value as a cryptocurrency, and businesses are beginning to access Ether as a form of payment. Also, there is no person, bank or government that can claim that it can prevent Ethereum from inflation. Below are some of the factors that makes Ethereum valuable:

1. Sovereignty

All transactions on Ethereum platform are normally validated to ensure they are valid. A number of factors are to be considered for a transaction to be termed as valid, but the basic one is that the account must have a balance greater than the amount the user is sending. There is no purpose or need behind why the user is sending Ether. Any Ethereum user is allowed to spend their coins the way they want without authorization. In the case of developed countries, it may seem unnecessary to have control over your wealth, but it is of great importance in developing countries where national currencies are constantly affected by inflation. Having a cryptocurrency such as Ethereum helps such users untie from their fiat currency. The good thing with Ethereum is that users can get complete sovereignty if they wish, something not provided in the fiat currency system. In Ethereum, users may choose to involve and trust third parties, but this is not a must as is the case with fiat currencies.

2. Mathematics and Scarcity

The Ethereum platform is governed by mathematical laws. In the case of fiat currency, a central bank and a government can regulate the supply of money. The coin distribution for Ethereum is written into an immutable code made available to the public, and an agreement is reached through a consensus. Ethereum, which is a digital asset, is backed up by an unbreakable encryption and mathematical truths, which is not the case with fiat currency system.

Ethereum is an inflationary currency since 5 new Ethers are added to circulation once a new block is discovered. A new block is found around every 15 seconds. The supply of Bitcoin has a maximum limit of 21 million bitcoins. However, there is no limit to the amount of Ether that can be found in circulation at any point in time. However, in an effort to curb inflation, it is expected that the amount of Ether that gets into circulation after the discovery of a new valid block, currently 5 Ethers, will reduce.

3. Liquidity

Ether has real value in constant demand throughout the world. Most exchanges are now able to complete many Ether transactions within seconds without having to move the price. It may have high liquidity, but its users have said that they like it, as it makes it easy for them to convert between Ethereum and fiat currencies. Ethereum is said to be one of the cryptocurrencies with a high liquidity, meaning that it is easy to convert it to any other coin, a crypt-coin or fiat currency at any time. This is possible despite your location. The process has been easy due to the sprouting of many online cryptocurrency exchanges. For some cryptocurrencies, you are first required to convert them into a particular cryptocurrency then into fiat currency. This involves a lot of bureaucracy which most users do not like. This is not the case with Ethereum as it is more liquid, making it more valuable.

4. Efficiency

Ethereum transactions are well known for their speed and being cheap. The network is capable of handling 15 transactions every second. The protocol is expected to be upgraded so that this figure may increase even to 1000+ transactions. With Ethereum transactions, no third party verification is needed, which explains why Ethereum transactions run faster. In the case of fiat currencies, a bank or other third party may need days to do the verification, which slows transactions. The involvement of a third party in a transaction also leads to reduced security and an increase in the transaction fee. This is not the case with the Ethereum blockchain, hence it has increased the magnitude of the network in terms of the number of transactions that can be handled.

These are the factors have made Ethereum special. Its token, Ether, which fuels the network, is now being accepted by a number of merchants as a means of payment. This means that you can buy items from such merchants with Ether in the same way that you would buy with fiat currency such as US dollars. However, not so many merchants are accepting cryptocurrencies as a means of payments. The number is expected to increase as the popularity and adoption of cryptocurrencies increase.

For any cryptocurrency to gain value, the number of people using it must increase. More people means an increase in the value of the cryptocurrency. Ethereum offers a number of benefits compared to other cryptocurrencies, including the provision of smart contracts discussed previously. Due to this, the popularity of Ethereum is expected to increase, and its value is expected to rise even more. This means that smart contracts add value to Ethereum. The fact that Ethereum provides its users with tools for developing decentralized applications makes it unique, giving it even more value. This feature is not offered by other cryptocurrencies and blockchain implementations. Cryptocurrencies such as

Bitcoin are only used as a means of facilitating peer-to-peer payments between transacting parties. Ethereum has gone a step further to provide its users with tools to develop blockchain applications and run them on the same platform.

Since Ether has value, you can use it to buy items at a number of selected online stores. There is no way for you to print Ether and carry it in the form of notes. It is only available in the form of a code and balances. To pay, you have to transfer the Ether from your wallet to where the merchant requires. In most cases, you may be required to send the Ether to an exchange that has been tasked with the responsibility of collecting payments by the merchant. The merchant will know how to get the money from the exchange to his own wallet. This means that you should not expect to carry Ether in the form of printed money.

Chapter 2- Getting Started with Ethereum

The first step to begin using Ethereum is to create an Ethereum account. The creation of an Ethereum account simply involves the creation of a wallet, which is the storage you will be using to store your Ether. You can easily do this using the Mist Ethereum Wallet. This is an application through which you can interact with several Ethereum accounts. It is a free Ethereum wallet application that is easy to use by anyone.

The following steps will help you create an Ethereum wallet on MyEtherWallet:

1. On your browser, open MyEtherWallet.com.

2. Ensure that you are in the tab for "Generate Wallet".

3. You will see the field where you are required to enter a password for the account. Type a strong password for the wallet in the field, then click "Generate Wallet".

4. If the creation of the wallet runs successfully, you will see a success message. This means that the wallet has been generated successfully.

To ensure that the Ether you keep in the wallet is secure, it is recommended that you keep only the keystore file and the address. The unencrypted private key should be disregarded as well as the unencrypted JSON file.

It would also be good for you to print a paper wallet and ensure that there aren't electronic copies of the key on your computer. To send Ether from your MyEtherWallet account, you just open your account, then click the "Send Ether & Tokens" tab.

You will then have two methods of accessing your Ethereum account. First, you can use the KeyStore File and secondly you can use Private Key. To use the first option, ensure that you have checked the "Keystore File (UTC/JSON)" option. On your right, click the option for "SELECT WALLET FILE..." You will be prompted to type a password for your encrypted keystore file.

Other than the above method, you can opt to choose a "Private Key". You only have to choose the "Private Key" option then you paste your private key to unlock the wallet. After pasting the private key, click the "Unlock" button.

You will then be required to specify the address of the recipient as well as the amount of Ether you need to send. Note that the "Gas Limit" allows you to specify the maximum amount of fee that the transaction is going to spend. If you set it to a low amount, there is a high chance that the transaction will fail, so be aware of this. You can then send the transaction and the Ether will be send to the recipient specified. If you notice that the transaction fails, you may have to increase the value of the gas limit.

If you need to create an account on Mist Ethereum Wallet, you will be allowed to create a password for your account. Ensure that you keep this password so that it is not stolen. Also, note that there is no option for recovering the password once lost, so ensure that you don't forget it. The account will be created and will initially have a balance of zero Ether. You will be able to see the details of the account and the public address should be noted well.

You can also create an Ethereum account via the command line. Begin by installing GETH, which is a GO Ethereum client. To create a new account, run the following command on the command line:

geth account new

Type in a password for the account, ensuring that you can easily memorize it as there is no way of recovering it. Feel free to create as many accounts as you want and whenever you want to view them, run the command:

geth account list

Once you have created the account, its public address will be printed. This is the address you should give to others who may need to send you some Ether.

Chapter 3- Buying and Selling Ethereum

Buying Ethereum

Most people have tried to acquire Ethereum through mining, but they have found it to be hard. The best and easiest way to acquire Ethereum is by buying it.

Ethereum (ETH) vs. Ethereum Classic (ETC)

The Ethereum classic is a cryptocurrency created after a disagreement with the way the original Ethereum conducts its business. This happened after a hacker managed to hack the system and steal Ethereum worth $60m. The Eth supporters said that the code should be modified and the stolen coins refunded, while the ETC supporters argued that "code is law" and whatever happened has happened. What happened after that was that ETC maintained the original Ethereum code while the ETH forked the code in order to create a new Ethereum.

This led to the presence of two competing cryptocurrencies but with different exchange rates. Today, the price of ETH is a bit higher and has been made much available to the cryptocurrency community, making it more accessible.

Buying Ethereum on an Exchange

If you are buying Ether for the first time, it is recommended that you do it from an exchange. The transaction will do all the work for you as well as the hard transaction.

The process of buying Ether is determined by the country you are in and the currency you have. You should find someone with Ether who needs to trade it for another currency. You can find the person online or in person.

People living in cities such as Toronto and New York are lucky, as there are Ether meet ups in which you can get someone from whom to buy Ether. However, this option is not available for those living in less populated cities. In such cases, you can rely on an exchange from where you will exchange your currency for Ether. On most exchanges, you are allowed to buy Ether with your bitcoins or US dollars. Typically, you have to go through a sign-up process, but be sure no personal details are asked.

To buy when using another currency, you may be required to go through a number of steps. Bitcoin forms the most popular cryptocurrency in the world, hence people in the world want you to use it when trading. This means that if you have rubles and you need to purchase Ether, you should first purchase bitcoins from an exchange, then use the bitcoins to purchase the Ether.

The following steps will help you purchase Ethereum:

1. Sign up for an Account at an Exchange

Just like he other cryptocurrencies, you can buy and sell Ethereum on an online exchange. There are various such services considered to be highly reputable. Examples of the popular exchanges include Kraken, Coinbase, Bitstamp and Gemini. Before buying Ethereum, choose one of these exchanges and create an account.

2. Verify your Account

Most exchanges require you to verify your account through one or many ways. You may be required to upload some documents to prove your identity. The period taken to verify your account varies from one exchange to another depending on how busy it, but in most cases, it takes one or two days.

3. Deposit Fiat Currency

You will then be required to deposit your fiat money into the account you have just created on the exchange. The transfer can be done from a bank account or Wire Transfer to the exchange. It may take some days for the money to reflect on the exchange, but this varies from exchange to exchange.

4. Begin the Trade

Now that you have an already verified account with a balance on it, you can purchase Ether or any other cryptocurrency from your exchange account. The exchanges operate differently, but you must verify or confirm transactions and give time for the processing of the transaction. The processing time can be determined by the number of transactions pending othatr you have requested.

5. Withdraw Ether to the Wallet

When you have kept your Ether on the exchange, you are not exercising direct control over it. It is recommended that you withdraw the Ether from the exchange to a wallet over which you exercise full control. Exchanges are more exposed to hacker attacks, hence we don't recommend keeping your Ether there. We recommend you download then install an Ethereum wallet and use it for the storage of your Ether. You will have to provide the account address of your wallet on the exchange in order to transfer the Ether to the wallet. However, avoid using the private code and the password on the exchange as this may expose them to hackers who may, in turn, hack into your wallet. If you need to trade the Ether again, you will have to transfer it from the wallet to the exchange. A fee for doing this may be charged, but it is always insignificant. It is better to incur an insignificant fee rather than exposing all your Ether to hackers.

Buying Ethereum via Peer-to-Peer Trade

If you don't want to buy Ethereum from an exchange, maybe because of the technical steps involved, you can choose to do it through a direct or peer-to-peer trade. This will give you a say in terms of where the Ethereum comes from. Through a direct trade, you are able to set up and plan how to transact with the seller you prefer.

One of the main advantages of buying Ethereum through a direct trade is that you must not use your bank account to buy Ethereum. This is good for the security of money in your bank account. On sites such as LocalEthereum, you are allowed to use your Amazon gift cards, PayPal or even cash. Note that direct trades for Ethereum are still new, hence we recommend that you only choose LocalEthereum.

Open the homepage for LocalEthereum, then browse through all the offers available. Different people from all over the world will be selling their Ethereum at different prices, but you can filter the sellers by factors such as payment method, location, etc. You can spot a deal that fits you and go with it. You can compare their rate with active trading rates on sites such as CryptoCompare, LiveCoinWatch, etc. If you are happy with the rate offered by a particular seller, just click the "Buy" button located on the right side of the screen.

To proceed with the purchase, you will be required to create an account, but this is not a lengthy process and no verification is needed as in the case of exchanges. You will then go through a conversation with the seller, which is normally encrypted. During the conversation, discuss and explore the terms of the deal. If the seller is okay with the terms, he or she will transfer the Ether to an escrow account, and you will be required to make a payment for the Ether via the method you choose. Once the payment is done successfully, the Ether will be released to your wallet of choice.

Privacy and Security

LocalEthereum provides a good level of privacy in that after completion of a transaction, your unique, private key will destruct in order to invalidate the message history. However, it may happen in the middle of the transaction that one of the involved parties is not happy. In such a case, an arbitrator comes in to help and goes through all the messages exchanged between the two parties.

The platform provides a platform where a peer-to-peer trade can be carried out. This means that the site does not suffer from slowdowns that usually happen when carrying out lengthy trades. It also means that there are no crashes that normally result from heavy trading periods. However, the transfer of Ether may still take a longer period of time, but there is no need to worry about the currency being locked up if the site is not accessible.

If you decide to do an in-person trade for cash or any other medium, ensure that you take the necessary precautions when meeting a stranger. Ensure that you meet in a public place that is well-lit. It is unlikely that you will encounter anything strange, but it is hard to predict the intentions of a stranger.

Purchasing Ethereum Anonymously

One may choose to remain anonymous when purchasing Ethereum for a number of reasons. Some countries do not allow it, but it is still possible for you to do so through an online peer-to-peer exchange such as LocalBitcoins.com.

You will first be required to purchase bitcoins, then exchange them for Ether. You must have a Bitcoin wallet. You can then exchange the Bitcoin for Ether anonymously via ShapeShift.io. However, note that there is a restriction in terms of the maximum amount you can transact each time.

Selling Ethereum

You may have Ether but you need to buy an item from a vendor who does not accept Ethereum as a means of payment. In such a case, you should sell your Ether and get other forms of currencies, even fiat currencies. This is possible.

The best way to sell your Ether is through an exchange that offers an ETH/USD pairing. A good example is Coinbase which provides both mobile and web interfaces that can be used for selling Ether. You must create a Coinbase account then provide details of your bank account. After that, transfer your Ethereum from your wallet to the Coinbase account/wallet.

Next, click the "Accounts" tab, then click "Receive" button. The address to which you can send the funds will be shown. Now that the Ethereum is in your Coinbase wallet, click "Buy/Sell" tab. Click "Sell" option, then set the currency to "Ethereum". You will be required to specify the amount of Ethereum you need to sell and then confirm the transaction.

Other than Coinbase, you can also sell your Ethereum for USD on Gemini. This platform is only available in a web version and it is a bit complicated compared to Coinbase. The exchange requires you to first create an account, then link it to your bank account. Next, you will have to transfer your Eth to the platform then sell it from there. The amount of fee charged for the sale is determined by a schedule.

You can also sell your Eth on Kraken. They also require you to create an account and connect it to your bank account. You are required to verify your account by providing details such as full name, country of residence, date of birth and phone number.

After that, you can transfer your Eth to the Kraken account then sell it from there.

Chapter 4- Ethereum Wallets

Once you have acquired Ether, you need to look for a way of storing it safely. This may not sound serious, but it is possible to lose your coins. Note that once you have lost your coins, it is impossible to recover them.

Ethereum as well as other cryptocurrencies are stored in cryptocurrency wallets. These wallets are similar to your bank account. The wallet is identified by a public address and a private key. The public address is used when others want to send you Ether. It is like an account number. The private key is used to authorize payments from your wallet. It acts like an ATM PIN.

You can disclose the public address to others, but the private key should always be kept secret. Buyers must use your public address whenever they need to send Ether to you. You are the only person who should know the private key. Anyone who knows your private key can use the Ether kept in your wallet. Also, note that there is no way for you to recover the private key. Once lost, all the Ether in the wallet will be lost. You must come up with a secure and safe way of storing the private key.

There are various types of Ethereum wallets. The kind of wallet to use is determined by accessibility and security.

Different types of wallets offer different levels of security. Let us discuss the various wallets that can be used for storage of Ethereum:

Mobile Wallets

These light clients require less data to download and connect to the network, then use for making transactions. This makes them suitable for mobile clients and convenient, but they are not safe for the storage of Ether. With full Ethereum clients, one gets a more secure way of receiving transactions since there is no need to trust the nodes or miners in order to send them an accurate information, but they themselves validate the transactions.

The storage of private keys on a device that has been detached from the Internet (a process called "cold storage") is the best way to store Ether since it is very hard to hack. However, the process is difficult to use especially in cases where the Ether has been stored on a smartphone or computer connected to the Internet.

Hardware Wallets

These small wallets are the best option for the storage of Ether. It is possible to detach hardware wallets from the Internet, and you can even sign Ether transactions without the need to be online. However, since hardware wallets function like a deposit box, they are not a good option if you will need to use Ether frequently or when traveling.

Desktop Wallets

These wallets run on a laptop or PC. You can download an Ethereum client, which is a copy of a whole Ethereum blockchain. Note that Ethereum clients are of different types since they are developed in different programming languages. These clients also differ in terms of performance. The process may take a number of days and it increases with the growth of Ethereum. The wallet should be kept in sync with latest transactions on the blockchain.

Paper Wallets

This is another cold storage option that involves writing the private key on a piece of paper or printing it, then locking it in a secure place such as a deposit box. You can use online tools to generate the key pairs directly into your computer, but the servers of the website are not secure as the keys can be stolen if the website is hacked.

You can also use the command to generate the keys, but you should have the right cryptographic packages installed for the language you prefer. Note that if the private key is lost, it will be lost for good. This means that you should make several copies of the private key and keep them in different secure locations so that if one is lost or damaged, you can use the other one.

Chapter 5- Ethereum Mining

Miners plays a very important role on the Ethereum platform to ensure that the blockchain works in the right way. The role of the miners on the Ethereum platform is to generate Ether in such a way that no central issuer is required. In Ethereum, Ether is generated through mining at a rate of 5 Ethers for every mined block. Other than generating Ether, mining plays another important role.

Banks are normally responsible for recordkeeping and retaining what happens during transactions. They also ensure that money is not created from anywhere, and that users do not cheat to be able to spend their money more than once. Blockchain has introduced a kind of ledger in which all transactions are recorded and verified by the users on the network instead of having an intermediary do so.

The goal is to have a trustless or a trust-minimizing monetary system, but it is still good for the records to be secured to ensure no one cheats. Mining makes it possible to have decentralized recordkeeping. The miners must come to a consensus about the record history and they avoid fraud. This is a problem that had not been solved in the decentralized currencies before the proof-of-work blockchains.

How Ethereum Mining Works

Today, the process of mining Ethereum is similar to the process of mining Bitcoin. For every block of transactions, the miners use their computers to guess answers to the puzzle until one of the miners wins.

In most cases, the users are expected to run the unique header metadata of the block through a hash function, which then gives a fixed-length string of numbers and letters. To ensure that each time a different hash value is obtained, the value of the nonce is varied each time. If any miner finds a block whose hash matches the target hash, he is rewarded with Ether and he broadcasts a message on the network so that other miners will stop solving the block. The block is also broadcast to miners so they may validate it and add it to their ledger of transactions. Once the hash for a block is found, all other miners stop working on it, and they proceed to work on the next block.

It is hard for miners to cheat in Ethereum mining. There is no way you can fake the work then find the correct answer for the puzzle. This is why the method for solving the puzzle is known as *proof-of-work*. The process of verifying the hash takes a very short time.

However, note that the supply of Ether is not infinite. Control of the amount of Ether on the network was decided in a 2014 presale. The amount of Ether issues each year cannot exceed 18 million. This mechanism is employed to reduce on inflation.

Each block should have a proof-of-work of a particular difficulty to be validated into a consensus. The algorithm responsible for validation of the blocks is known as Ethash. It is responsible for taking the nonce input and mapping it to a result below a threshold which is specified as a way of controlling the difficulty. If the difficulty is manipulated, the miner will be able to control the amount of time required to find a new block.

The difficulty has to be manipulated frequently to ensure that the network produces only one block after every 12 seconds. You can mine Ethereum from the comfort of your home. Knowledge of how to write scripts and use the command prompt is needed. The process becomes much easier once it has been broken down into manageable steps.

A lot of electricity is consumed during Ethereum mining. However, in return, if the mining process is done efficiently, one can generate much income from the process. There are Ethereum calculators available for the purpose of calculating profits in Ethereum mining. This means that you don't have to get worked up as you will earn a profit at the end of the process.

As more miners join the platform, the process of mining Ethereum becomes harder. The competition is high, hence one requires high computing power to be able to mine Ethereum. If your computer has a slow speed, you may end up not earning anything from Ethereum mining.

Shift to proof of stake

It is now believed that Ethereum may not require miners forever. Its developers are planning to do away with the proof-of-work algorithm normally used for verifying the valid blocks. In the proof-of-stake system, the network will be protected by the token owners. When the proof-of-stake is implemented, it will help developers and users achieve a way of reaching consensus without consuming many resources.

Selecting Mining Hardware

Before getting started, you must have a computer dedicated only to mining. There exists two types of mining hardware: CPUs and GPUs. Mining GPUs is a bit faster, which means that one can guess answers to the puzzles quickly. Currently, you can only mine Ether with GPUs.

The process of setting up a GPU can be a complex task and I recommend that you choose the best type of GPU from the available options. The choice should be based on hash rate performance, initial cost of the card as well as power consumption. It is good for you to set up a mining rig, a machine made up of several GPUs, but it may take you up to a week to set one up.

You can also use a profit calculator to know the amount of Ether you can earn at a particular hash rate. You will be able to know whether that hash is enough to cover for electricity costs as well as other costs associated with Ethereum mining and still be left with some profit. In Bitcoin, there are power ASICs that can be used successfully in Bitcoin mining. However, there are no powerful ASICs that can be used for Ethereum mining.

The Mining Software

Once you have selected the hardware to use for mining, you should install the software. The miners should first install a client that will help them connect to the network. If you are a programmer who likes using the command line, you can install *Geth*. This can run an Ethereum node written in Go programming language.

Begin by downloading Geth, then follow the necessary instructions based on the operating system you are using. You can find Geth on GitHub by clicking this link: https://github.com/Ethereum/go-Ethereum/releases. After the download, unzip the package then run it.

Once you have installed Geth, your node will be able to talk to the other nodes on the network, meaning that it will be connected to the Ethereum network. Geth will also provide you with an interface thorugh which you can deploy smart contracts and send transactions by use of the command line.

You can mine test on your own private network and experiment with smart contracts and decentralized applications. To mine on a test network, you are not required to have fancy hardware, but can use your computer and install Geth. You can also use other client software.

Install Ethminer

For you to mine real Ether, you should install a real mining software. At this point, you have downloaded the client and it is part of the network, so you can now download the Ethminer. Make sure you download the right one based on the operating system you are running. After it has been installed, your node will be tasked with the responsibility of securing your network.

Join a Mining Pool

Mining Ether on your own might be tough. Miners usually combine their mining power into "mining pools" to increase their chances of solving cryptographic puzzles and earning Ether. The profits earned from such a mining process are shared on the basis of the amount of power one has contributed.

There are a number of factors involved when joining a mining pool. Every pool may not be available forever, and the power of computation of each pool keeps changing, so a number of factors should be considered when choosing a pool to join. Note that mining pools do not have same payout structures.

To join a mining pool, you will be taken through a signup process on a website before being allowed to join the pool and begin mining Ether. Again, it will be good for you to stay updated with what is current on the market as new Ethereum mining tools are discovered on a yearly basis.

Ensure that your hard disk has enough space, probably around 30GB. This is enough for the blockchain.

Just like Bitcoin, Ethereum relies on the Proof of Work (PoW) system. It involves solving complex equations, and miners have to clear or meet this so that their blocks can be added to the blockchain. The system has an impact on the environment and consumes too much electricity. However, with the use of Dagger Hashimoto algorithm, individuals can mine Ethereum on their home computers and they will incur a minimal expenditure. However, there are plans for the process of mining Ethereum to be replaced completely by a mechanism known as Proof of Stake, and a consensus algorithm will be powering this. The Ethereum network is simply a string of connections which is maintained by computers, with an undeniable impact and good profit.

Chapter 6- Ethereum for Investment

Ethereum is one of the cryptocurrencies that have taken the world by storm. It is a decentralized system that allows payments to be sent without having to involve a bank or any other third party. Since its release, Ethereum has established itself as the second largest cryptocurrency in the world. Many people have been attracted by this cryptocurrency, especially because it is possible to run third-party applications on this network.

Digital currencies such as Ethereum have the potential of changing the financial industries in the same way that Uber changed the transport industry. People are less likely to trust the traditional finance industry, hence they are turning to the online world. Ethereum is tradable on various exchanges. There are many exchanges online where you can trade Ethereum and even exchange it for other currencies, including fiat currencies. These exchanges provide excellent customer services and any coin you may need.

A high number of organizations across the world are now accepting Bitcoin as a form of payment. The number of companies embracing Ether is also expected to increase as more people begin to adopt cryptocurrencies. This makes Ethereum a good investment choice.

Note that Ethereum, just like Bitcoin, is a volatile cryptocurrency. Its value goes up and down, but this is normal even with regular currencies like the USD. This means that it is possible to make a loss or a profit from an Ethereum investment. The good thing is that there are several ways you can invest in Ethereum other than trading it alone. If trading Ethereum is not for you, then you can choose other ways of investing in this cryptocurrency. Let us discuss the various ways you can invest in Ethereum:

Buying and Holding Ethereum

You can venture into buying and holding Ethereum as a form of investment. Take advantage of the high volatility of Ethereum to buy it when its price goes down and sell it when the price goes up. You will earn a profit from the difference between the selling price and buying price. However, you should be good at speculating about the direction in which the price will move. There are various charts online from which you can extract the price patterns of Ethereum and these can help you predict the direction in the future. It is also expected that mobile and desktop applications that will help in predicting the price movement of Ethereum will be developed in the future.

This will make this type of investment very easy to venture into.

Trading Ethereum

There are a number of exchanges on which you can get a platform to trade crypto assets. Examples include GDAX and Poloniex. In this case, you are allowed to trade the Ether you have with the other crypto assets such as cryptocurrencies. The good thing is that there are numerous cryptocurrencies for which you can trade your Ether.

Buying and Diversifying

You can buy Ethereum and exchange it for the other cryptocurrencies like Ripple and Litecoin. In any case one of the coins fails, you will be protected.

Mining Ethereum

Ethereum mining is a good investment opportunity. You can buy all the hardware equipment necessary for mining Ethereum. After that, you can setup the software for mining Ethereum and you will be ready to begin mining

Ethereum. The Ether you earn as reward can be sold in exchange for fiat currency.

Note that Ether is a currency and you should treat it like that as an investor. Shares of Ether are not bought in the same way as ETFs or stocks. You only hope that people on the Internet will pay you more for the Ether tokens than the amount for which you had bought them.

Chapter 7- Securing Ethereum

You must ensure that your Ether is kept securely so that hackers do not access it. The Ethereum wallet is the most essential component in the network and it should be kept safely. It is the one that holds your Ether, hence it is similar to a real wallet in which you store your money.

Just like a real wallet, the Ethereum wallet can be stolen. Due to this, it should not be left on a device that is accessed frequently or connected to the Internet, as you risk being hacked. Once an Ethereum wallet is stolen, there is no means to recover it; the courts cannot help you recover it, and it is impossible to reverse what has happened. There are a number of ways through which you can secure your Ethereum wallet and Ether.

1. Hardware Wallet

The use of a hardware wallet is one of the best ways of ensuring that your Ether is safe. The hardware wallet generates a private key and stores it offline. The offline storage is not connected to any other device that is connected to the Internet, making it hard for hackers to access the key. When Ethereum coins are kept offline, they are protected against digital theft, which is a major threat to cypto-coins. When creating an offline Ethereum wallet, you are provided with a recovery seed, and a PIN is provided that will secure access to the device. Both the recovery seed and the PIN should be secured well, since access may lead to loss of funds.

There are various types of Ethereum hardware wallets you can use. However, the most popular are Trezor and Ledger Nano S. To keep your Ethereum on a Trezor device, you should combine it with MyEtherWallet. This means that there is some bureaucracy involved when using it, and this is why most people prefer to use Ledger Nano S. A paper wallet is also a good way of securing your Ether. This involves printing the private key on a piece of paper and storing it in a safe place.

2. 2 Factor Authentication

You may store your Ether on a hardware, mobile or desktop wallet, or even on an exchange, but 2-factor authentication should always be implemented whatever the kind of storage used. It is a good way of protecting your Ether as it offers an additional security layer. The 2FA works by requiring the user to provide a one- time password (OTP) before they can log into the wallet or even send Ether. The Google Authenticator provides an interface, and a number of Ethereum wallets are using it for authentication purposes.

Various wallets implement the 2FA feature in different ways. However, despite the kind of implementation, 2FA provides the same layer of security. For a hacker or any thief to gain access to your wallet, they will need to have the password as well as access to the physical device on which the OTP will be generated or sent.

The implementation of 2FA using an app such as Google Authenticator has proved to be an excellent way of providing an extra layer of security. Other platforms have chosen not to use an app such as this, but they bypass it and send the OTP in the form of an SMS (Short Message Service). This should be avoided since a potential hacker can easily observe the OTP without having to unlock the phone. You may be aware of what conmen do to con and trick telecom operators to redirect a phone number to another SIM card. This can be catastrophic in case they succeed in doing this to your SIM card, as all your Ether may end up being lost. This is because the attacker will be able to gain access to any platform protected via 2FA.

3. Multi Signature Wallets

These are wallets in which multiple participants are required to sign transactions as a way of protecting the Ether kept in the wallet. Most multi signature wallets operate on the "2 of 3" protocol in which 2 of the 3 private keys have to sign the transaction. It is only after this that the transaction can be broadcast to the network. For security purposes, these three keys should not be kept in a single location to prevent a single point of attack. If they are kept in a single location, an attacker who gains access to the location will get the keys and use them to sign a transaction.

Different wallets also use different implementations of the multi-signature wallet feature. In other cases, the users are able to agree on the number of private keys that must sign a transaction before it is broadcast to the network. This must always be true for a transaction to run successfully. The only problem with this type of implementation is that a number of users may agree to sign a transaction as a way of defrauding other users.

4. Strong diversification

Storage of all the Ether you have in a single location is always not recommended. It is better to diversify the places you store your Ether. You can keep some of it in bank safety deposit box, some in a safe in your home and some in a safe house. In case any of these locations is accessed by a thief, you will be safe from having all your Ether being stolen.

5. Separate the ERC20 Tokens

After separating the ERC20 tokens from Ether holdings, it becomes easy for you to create a paper wallet. An additional layer of security is created in that it becomes easy for you to send Ether tokens to the paper wallet. However, to send the Ether from the wallet, you are expected to have some amount of Ether in your wallet so that it can be used for the transaction fee.

This will be the fee or the gas required to run the transaction. This means that if your wallet has no gas, you will be required to go a step further to get the money out of the wallet. If a potential thief knows nothing about the ERC20 tokens, he will only have to scan the wallet for the Ether.

The security mechanism you choose for your Ether will be determined by the degree of risk you are ready to tolerate. You should use all the information discussed above as a guide when choosing ways to secure your Ether. It is true that people have lost their crypto-coins. However, these losses have not been from the failure of the underlying blockchain technology, but from user mistakes and ignorance. You should take responsibility for the security of your Ether tokens by ensuring that you have direct and total control over your wallet.

To maximize the security of your Ether, avoid keeping it in online storages such as exchanges. These are connected to the Internet, making it easy for hackers and other thieves to access. Offline means of storage such as hardware wallets are recommended. Also, avoid storing all your Ether in a single storage location.

Chapter 8- Developing Dapps on the Ethereum Platform

Since its initial release, Ethereum has spawned an ecosystem of thinkers, developers and entrepreneurs all of whom want to tap into the potential of this blockchain technology. The number of decentralized applications running on the Ethereum platform is increasing every day. On Ethereum, people can use blockchain technology to develop decentralized applications. A decentralized application is simply an application that serves a particular purpose without having to depend on a third party. Through a decentralized application, users from different sides can communicate without having to depend on a centralized party to facilitate the interaction.

A Dapp goes beyond providing a front end to users to perform particular tasks, but it goes ahead to connect users from different sides. In the case of centralized applications, some tasks are left with a centralized authority. Examples of such tasks include escrow protection, identity management and filtering. In Ethereum, such tasks are left to the network or some of the trusted nodes in the network.

A decentralized application is made up of two parts, the frontend and the backend. The frontend is written in

HTML, while the backend is the database. The frontend part has full network access, so you can continue using Bootstrap or any other framework you like. The process of developing the frontend for a Dapp is similar to the development of a website. Reactive programming can be used by using the callback functions, meaning there is no need for you to learn a new framework.

Ethereum Environment Setup

Alethzero is the C++ implementation of Ethereum deigned to be used by developers. We will install the "master" version of Alethzero due to it stability and the fact that it has all the latest features.

Download the binaries for Alethzero based on the operating system you are using.

Next, you should install MIX. This will be used as the integrated development environment (IDE). You should finally install Mist, which will provide you with an environment for testing your Dapp and fine tuning the frontend during the development process.

Once you start Alethzero, you will be presented with a number of interfaces. Your resolution may vary, and you may not see all the interfaces. Just click the "X" to close all the panes manually, resize the screen to fit your resolution, then read the interfaces manually by right clicking below the title bar and the right of the "refresh" button.

At the center of the screen, you should see a browser window, forming the Webkit view. The exiting web can be browsed from there. You can try something like Facebook. The other panels have some technical and debug information. This interface may not be friendly to users, but it is very useful to developers. The final Ethereum browser is named "Mist" and building on top of Go Ethereum implementation will provide a different look and feel.

Note that the Ethereum platform is generalized and can be used for building financial applications, games, social networks, gambling applications and other types of applications. We will write a simple contract which functions like a bank. However, this will have a transparent ledger that can be viewed by the whole world. We will issue a number of tokens, then send them to friends. In the web 2 world, this app would be implemented in PHP and MySQL, but users should trust you as an honest individual, that always keeps a consistent ledger, such that hackers cannot break into your server;

plus, you have honest employees who cannot plant a backdoor.

Understanding the Gas

The "gas" is an important concept which will help you master the Ethereum smart contracts. The decentralized web should be powered to keep on running. Ethereum cannot work under the reliance of any centralized authority. This is because the authority may end up manipulating the database. Instead of this, each node in the network holds a copy of the decentralized database and they can audit it.

The nodes of the network process the code being executed in the database and they vote to come to an agreement regarding the correct state of the database. The majority vote wins, and the nodes are incentivized to do the verification. The voting is normally done at regular intervals, most after every 12.7 seconds. The contract we have written will be stored in the database. It will be triggered then executed once other users or the other contracts call it.

This approach has a limitation in terms of processing speed. The total processing power of the Ethereum network, regardless of total number of nodes forming it, is small. This is why you should not store megabytes of data in the Ethereum network or render your 3d graphics. However, new mechanisms for doing this are under implementation.

Also, due to the limited computation power, the right measurement should be done so that a single actor doesn't commit evil deeds like running infinite loops on the Ethereum nodes. This measurement is done using a unit called "gas".

For a function to be executed, gas is needed. When calling a function, you should specify the coinsAmount of gas you will need to send to the contract, and the coinsAmount you need to pay for the gas, which is priced in Ether.

The various operations that a contract can support are normally priced differently. For example, a single execution can cost only one gas. Others, such as writing to the storage, normally cost more due to the fact that the storage is a scarce resource. In case much gas is sent to a contract and it doesn't use all of it, you will be refunded of the same. If little gas is sent to the contract, the contract will stop and roll back. The pricing of the gas is determined by the global consensus of the community. This is an indication that the operation whose gas is well priced will be executed first, then the rest will be executed later.

Chapter 9- Impact of Ethereum to the Economy

Cryptocurrencies are new innovations that can change the way the banking and entire finance industry operate. Ethereum is one of these cryptocurrencies that allows two parties to carry out a transaction without depending on a third party. It also provides its users with a platform on which they can develop decentralized applications. When transacting with Ether, the transactions are recorded, but information about the parties involved is not disclosed to the public. The transactions are verified and completed faster due to the fact that there is no reliance on third parties. At the same time, only a small fee is charged for Ether transactions. Banks have seen a huge potential in this technology to revolutionize the banking sector.

Ethereum as well as other cryptocurrencies have led to the emergence of new markets. It has led to the emergence of a new market unlike regular money under the control of some entity. Cyberspace is expected to rise and become the body that manages and handles such markets. The almost zero fee charged when using cryptocurrencies has made them superior to the traditional money we have been using. There are many benefits associated with Ethereum, and these are just a few.

Initially, all monetary transactions were enabled via the central banks. After the discovery of Ethereum and other cryptocurrencies, this changed. The power that was exclusively accorded to the central banks and governments has now shifted to the masses. The revolution in the way transactions are handled is impacting the economy in a huge way. To ensure adequate security and scrutiny, central banks and other financial institutions keep a record of all the transactions carried out. In the case of digital currencies, this economic may be challenged by individuals. Due to this, a new autonomous body capable of facilitating transactions has been created. If Ethereum and other cryptocurrencies are adopted on a large scale, it will lead to the politicization of money.

With traditional payment methods, such as credit and debit cards, high fees are charged. In most cases, the fee exceeds the cost of clearing the transaction. Also, it takes a long period of time for such transactions to be marked as complete. The adoption of Ethereum into business operations is expected to pressure the incumbents, such as credit and debit card companies, to improve. The fee cost is expected to be low or the appropriate one for accomplishing the transactions. They will need to compete with businesses that adopt payments through Ethereum, hence they will have to the reduce costs of carrying out transactions. This is good news for customers as the costs of transactions will go down. Cross-border payments are known to be charged at a high rate, and they take an exceptionally long time to complete. With Ethereum, such transactions can be carried out faster at a lower, almost negligible cost. Companies will need to compete with Ethereum by improving the old system.

Ethereum has made international transactions go faster. When making payments with the fiat currency, a centralized authority such as a bank must verify the transaction. The verification normally takes a number of days, which has slowed down international transactions. However, when paying with Ether, no centralized authority is expected to verify the transactions, and two parties can transact directly. This has provided a fast way of carrying out financial transactions at the international level. People who regularly make global payments can now smile as they will be able to carry out their transactions much faster than before.

Some companies are now tracking and recording their shipments via a blockchain. A good example of such a company is the Walmart test. Mangoes were tagged with numeric identifiers at the farm. Any time a new checkpoint was crossed from the farm to a broker to a distributor, their status was signed and logged. Other companies are now looking for ways to use the blockchain technology in their logistics. Maersk, a Danish shipping company is looking for ways to use blockchain in tracking shipments and coordinating with customs officials. Airbus, a jet manufacturing company in France, is looking for a way they can use the blockchain technology to track the many parts that go into building a jet.

Today, many projects using Ethereum are under development with ambitious goals. With Ethereum, the blockchain technology is expected to replace the stock market with peer-to-peer applications. Uber and Airbnb are expected to be bypassed with software so that vehicle owners and apartments can create a real sharing economy.

Consider the first Ethereum app, ICO (Initial Coin Offerings). These are now crowdfunding sales, with investors purchasing blockchain software known as *tokens*. These tokens can be used to represent an interest in a company or a share of future profit, or anything else. In 2017, blockchain entrepreneurs raised $750-million through ICOs. Two-thirds of these were raised via the Ethereum's ERC20-tokens, and the organization and projects on top of Ethereum are now worth billions.

Ethereum has created trust among people. Initially, people had no choice but to trust sovereign money. Money is simply a promissory note. With digital currencies such as Ethereum, this is not the case since trust is put in people. An individual who chooses to use a particular digital currency does so because he or she believes that it is money. It is not because they are told to use it as money.

Due to the use of digital money, new applications have been discovered. In the case of Ethereum, it has led to the discovery of smart contracts. When smart contracts are used together with digital money, they change the way deals are done. With smart contracts, procedures such as escrow protection are not necessary as one can specify when payments will be done by the use of conditions. This way, there is no need for intermediaries in carrying out financial transactions.

The current economy we are in has reached its peak potential. For us to develop further, a new era of economics is needed. The planetary resources we have currently are dwindling, and there is a need for a system with less emphasis on profit, but rather with a huge focus on the development of human resources. Virtual currencies are expected to bring in a new era of development and entrepreneurship. Ethereum has changed the way we do business today and has removed numerous bottlenecks when doing business.

Chapter 10- The Future of Ethereum Blockchain

Currently, Ethereum is changing a number of industries in the economy. However, its impact has not really been felt. While Ethereum is expected to change a number of sectors in the economy, its impact of has only been felt in the banking sector. However, Ethereum is expected to change operations in the other sectors of the economy.

Ethereum will lead to a reduction in identity theft. Once you give a credit card to a merchant, you give him or her access to your full credit line, even if the transaction is for a small amount. Credit cards normally operate on a "pull" basis, in which the store initiates payment and pulls the required amount from your account. Cryptocurrency uses the "push" mechanism in which the cryptocurrency holder sends exactly what he or she wants to a merchant or recipient with no further information. This means that it will be hard for any merchant to steal details that identify you directly.

Ethereum will reduce fraud because it is almost impossible to counterfeit cryptocurrencies. With fiat money, cases of fake notes in circulation in the economy are common. Ethereum is expected to solve this problem. With Ethereum, a sender cannot reverse a payment the way they want, but they are expected to go through a number of steps in which other users are involved. In other cases, it is impossible to reverse a transaction once a payment has been done. This will help in eliminating fraud. Also, it is hard to create fake Ether and have it circulate in the Ethereum network because the miners verifying the transactions on the network will easily detect this and flag it as counterfeit.

When purchasing real property, a lot of time is taken for settlement of the transaction. The reason is that a lot of third parties are involved, including lawyers, a notary. etc. A lot of delay and a high processing fee are typical. However, in Ethereum, a decentralized system, no third parties are required to carry out transactions. Ethereum is expected to change the real property industry so that the purchase and sale of property is carried out faster, more conveniently and at a lower cost.

Ethereum is also a platform on which one can develop applications, hence users will develop applications and contracts that don't require a third parties for approval, and such transactions will be carried out in a fraction the time and at a lower cost compared to the traditional way of doing things. The real property industry is full of conmen, and as a result, many have been defrauded.

Ethereum will increase trust in this field, attracting a high number of people to venture into the industry.

It is expensive for organizations, companies and institutions to carry out international payments. They spend huge sums of money to complete such transactions, and at the same time it takes a longer period of time for the transactions to be completed. These companies are waiting for an efficient way to reduce time and cost, and once invented they will all embrace it. Ethereum is expected to provide companies, mostly those in the financial sector, with an easy and cheap way of doing international payments and funds transfers. This way, the cost of carrying out transactions will be reduced. The funds saved from will be invested somewhere else. Financial institutions such as banks will attract an increased number of international customers since there would be a faster way of carrying out international transactions, while, and at the same, a lower fee is charged. Banks are expected to witness an increase in their number of customers. This will help boost the economy.

An increased number of businesses are expected to adopt Ethereum, which will bring in a new way of making payments. With Ethereum, transactions may be completed within a shorter period of time. This will have a great impact on the economy. When companies adopt a way of carrying out transactions faster, they will benefit a lot from the increase in earnings from such transactions. These businesses will be in a position to carry out a large number of transactions faster. This will lead to great customer satisfaction. At any particular point in time, there will be a limited number of transactions that a company can process. Internal transactions, which are very popular in financial institutions such as banks, will become easier and faster to process because the verification and confirmation will be done in a decentralized manner without queuing them to be verified by a centralized authority.

The popularity and rate of adoption of the Ethereum platform is growing rapidly. Many sectors of the economy are in need of establishing trust between transacting parties. Ethereum has a big advantage over other blockchain implementations in that it is one of the most trusted platform. The platform is expected to change how trust is established when new forms of establishing digital trust between transacting parties is established. This will lead to an increase in the popularity and adoption of the Ethereum blockchain since people are in need of assurance that their money, data and other assets are well secured.

There has been a rise in the number of Ethereum and other cryptocurrency markets; this has been a sideshow to the financial markets and the real economy. Ether prices and prices of other cryptocurrencies have gone high, and this is expected to increase further; but the expectation is that this should not have an impact on ordinary people.

However, companies who trade stocks publicly are making decisions that show they can benefit from cryptocurrencies, and the market is rewarding them hugely for them. If this trend continues, people who do not use Ethereum and other cryptocurrencies will suffer from a crypto bust. And a bust is expected to happen.

Companies will want to develop strategies based on proven principles so they can succeed. Application developers from all over the world will be empowered to can integrate cryptocurrencies in the applications they develop. There is an increase in the number of people using cryptocurrencies which will lead to the increased use of cryptocurrencies in the mainstream.

Chapter 11- Will Ethereum Overtake Bitcoin

Ethereum may well overtake Bitcoin. In Ethereum, blocks of transactions are created faster compared than happens in Bitcoin. Ethereum has also been found to be more efficient, hence it has a more decentralized future. ICOs have brought in something new to the cryptocurrency market, which has increased people's interest in blockchain technology, and this interest can scale very fast. Bitcoin has a total market supply of 21 million coins, and there are about 4x the number of Ethereum in circulation compared to Bitcoin. Currently, there are over 92 million Ethers in circulation. Ethereum is a large network compared to Bitcoin. Ethereum also provides another feature not available in Ethereum, that is, a platform on which we can run applications. This is why Ethereum is seen as the future of the blockchain technology.

Ethereum has introduced something new to the blockchain technology, that is, smart contracts. These have changed the blockchain technology from simply being a cryptocurrency. Blockchains are now a programmable platform, a type of trustable distributed computer that anyone can use to come up with an accountable institution. Bitcoin does not provide users with this kind of platform. In Ethereum, users are only expected to accept the right contracts to participate in these new institutions. Ethereum can be seen to have the same effect as the Web. After the invention of the Web, people were able to offer software as a service through browsers instead of having users buy disks and then install the software from them.

Bitcoin is well known for slow speed and high fees charged for transactions. This makes it unsuitable as a form of payment. You may be shocked to find that you are charged the same amount when paying for coffee as sending bitcoins worth $100,000. (This is a joke.)

Blockchain technologies that use smart contracts have great potential. Ethereum is one such blockchain implementations and its value dwarfs that of "store of value" chains. Platforms such as Ethereum are an operating system for decentralized commerce and finance.

Bitcoin can be seen as DOS while Ethereum can be seen as Windows or Mac OS. DOS came first and computers were largely using it. However, when Windows came into play, all computers shifted from DOS to Windows. That is what Ethereum is doing to Bitcoin. Most users are expected to shift from using Bitcoin to Ethereum. Note that Ethereum offers an advantage over Bitcoin in that it allows users to create their own applications on the platform, meaning they can create applications to meet specific needs. It is settled that Bitcoin is simply a currency.

The popularity of Ethereum is expected to rise in the same way that the Internet did in 2000s. New companies are being launched everyday with innovative business models and bleeding edge compliance with regulation. There is a need for new financing models. Bitcoin is one of the options that can help. However, many companies will not choose it due to the high fees involved in carrying out Bitcoin transactions.

Ethereum has shown dedication to innovation so that it can be the main platform for the development of blockchain applications in the future. Ethereum is also expected to grow, especially in terms of scalability so it can be a driver of future technology.

People and companies have shown their interest in the Initial Cost Offerings-based projects. For one to invest in these projects, they must first buy into Ethereum, and the terms of the contract will be applied automatically. Such situations are leading to an increase in the adoption of the Ethereum blockchain technology, and this could be very vital in the near future.

Other than being a cryptocurrency, Ethereum provides a platform for crowdfunding, contracts and other potential applications, meaning that Ethereum has provided something not previously available in the marketplace. When all these factors are combined, they give Ethereum staying power that other blockchain technologies do not have.

Ethereum faces minor issues of scalability. To enhance scalability, the proof-of-work algorithm has to be replaced by the proof-of-stake algorithm. In this new algorithm, voting will be based on the amount of tokens one owns. This algorithm is expected to make Ethereum even faster since the process of voting will have been made much easier. If this is implemented, Ethereum will become superfast and may replace Visa.

Chapter 12- Hard Forks

A hard fork is simply a change in the blockchain protocol. When a hard fork occurs, all previously invalid transactions and blocks are made valid, or vice versa. All the nodes on the network are then required to update the new version of the blockchain software. This means that during a hard fork, previously invalid transactions and blocks can be made valid, or previously valid blocks and transactions may be made invalid.

When a hard fork occurs, the blockchain permanently changes from one version to another, and the nodes running on the previous version of the blockchain cannot be accepted. After the occurrence of a hard fork in a blockchain, two paths are created. In one path, the nodes follow the new and updated version of the blockchain, while in the second path, the nodes follow the old and not updated version. A hard fork is very useful for a number of tasks including implementation or correction of important security risks found in the older versions of software, and the addition of new functions for the reversal of transactions.

A path of the blockchain is split by simply invalidating transactions that had been verified or confirmed by network nodes that have not been updated to the new version of the blockchain software. It is true that hacks may occur on a blockchain including the Ethereum blockchain. Cases of hackers gaining access to the systems have been reported. In such an occurrence, a hard fork can help in reversing all the transactions used to steal Ether from the network. This means that hard forks are a good way of recovering transactions.

In the cryptocurrency world, people are taking advantage of hard forks to create new altcoins. Developers are targeting hard forking in existing currencies instead of having to create their own from scratch. In the case of Ethereum, a good example is EtherZero. However, this fork was the result of a lack of community support and big platforms on which to trade it.

Hard forks were tried on Bitcoin in 2017. Bitcoin Cash and Bitcoin Gold are good examples of such forks, but Bitcoin Gold is much different from Bitcoin Cash and Bitcoin. Research has shown that this way of creating coins will have an effect on altcoins in the future. However, the process of taking an existing code and turning it into some new project is not new.

Ethereum was one of the first cryptocurrencies to receive hard forks because of the position that this cryptocurrency takes in the world, and people already like what it has to offer to users, hence they have want to create hard forks from it. If there is no good reason for creating a fork of the original codebase, then the fork is simply a money grab serving no real purpose. However, Ethereum Classic was not created in this way as it resulted from ideological differences between parts of the Ethereum community after the bailout of the DAO.

EtherZero is an Ethereum hard fork tried in 2018. However, most people are not aware that this project existed. The EtherZero fork was to take effect after the Ethereum network reached a block height of 4,936,270. However, the plans have already been cancelled.

The idea behind EtherZero was thrown out two weeks prior to its launch. This was good news to anyone in support of Ethereum as the project was expected to ruin the its reputation. The hard fork received little to no attention from the community, and no exchange was ready and willing to support the new coin. However, this did not come as a surprise as EtherZero was not expected to serve any purpose.

This does not indicate that the team has given up on developing and issuing EtherZero to users. Instead of using a hard fork, the team is now working on using an Initial Coin Offering (ICO). It is expected that a new name will be chosen in the near future, and rebranding of the same is expected to happen. However, no one can tell how this will be played, and only time will tell. The EtherZero website also looks unprofessional due to many spelling errors as well as other inconsistencies. However, there assurance that this project will be completed after well-organized scrutiny. It is believed that not much value will be gained after creating an Ethereum hard fork. The majority of such projects have no value and serve no purpose; thus they are not allowed to be traded on the major exchanges. It is a good to see the major trading platforms take such a stand on projects such as the EtherZero. We can conclude that people will stop creating hard forks of existing currencies with no real reason since it creates confusion.

The main question is, what is the effect of forks on the investors? Ethereum as a network, project and community has built up great good will, and there is a lower level of blood accompanying some of the hard forks of Bitcoin. The lack of division is an indication that there are fewer chances for any of these forks to gain serious support or traction across the sector.

Currently, these new tokens do not pose any major challenge or opportunities as there is no major way in which they can affect the price of ETH, and they do not influence the actions of the greater community. As a matter of surprise, many people are not aware that they even exist or have taken place. As things are currently, it is hard to tell how these will maintain any real value.

Ethereum forks are a representation of official upgrades made to the platform in an effort to helping the system scale effectively and be able to deal with the increase in activity of the network, or just secondhand solutions done by "lesser" development teams claiming to possess knowledge of how to implement more effective scaling solutions.

Other examples of Ethereum forks include Expanse (Exp), Shift (SHF) and Soil (SOIL). When mining these Ethereum forked altcoins, you can do it in the same way that you mine Ethereum with ethminer since they use the same algorithm as the original from which they have been forked.

Conclusion

This marks the end of this book. Ethereum is one of the many cryptocurrencies in the world. However, Ethereum has gone beyond being just a cryptocurrency because Ethereum offers users all the tools they need to develop and run decentralized applications. A decentralized application is simply an application that can run without relying on the control of a centralized authority. Ethereum supports the development and running of such applications. Ethereum has also introduced a feature known as *smart contracts*. In this feature, the developer writes a piece of code that will be executed when a particular condition is met. One can, for example, write a piece of code that will send some amount of Ether to an individual on a particular date. The sending of Ether will be done automatically when that date is reached without your interference.

The popularity of Ethereum is increasing on a daily basis because it offers a number of features that many institutions such as banks have been waiting for. For instance, Ethereum is expected to change the banking sector on a large scale. It will provide banks with a new way of establishing trust as well as a faster way of carrying out transactions. The amount of fees charged per transaction can also be reduced with the use of Ethereum.

Other than the banking sector, Ethereum is expected to change other sectors such as the real estate and stock trade industries. The rate at which Ethereum is adopted is expected to increase, hence it will increase the value of Ether, the token that fuels the Ethereum network.

www.ingramcontent.com/pod-product-compliance
Lightning Source LLC
Chambersburg PA
CBHW070207230526
45471CB00002B/856